SPACE OBJECTS

ASTEROIDS & METEORS

by Elizabeth Andrews

Cody Koala
An Imprint of Pop!
popbooksonline.com

Hello! My name is **Cody Koala**

This book is filled with videos, puzzles, games, and more! Scan the QR codes* while you read, or visit the website below to make this book pop.

popbooksonline.com/ast-met

*Scanning QR codes requires a web-enabled smart device with a QR code reader app and a camera.

abdobooks.com

Published by Pop!, a division of ABDO, PO Box 398166, Minneapolis, Minnesota 55439. Copyright ©2025 by Abdo Consulting Group, Inc. International copyrights reserved in all countries. No part of this book may be reproduced in any form without written permission from the publisher. Cody Koala™ is a trademark and logo of Pop!.

Printed in the United States of America, North Mankato, Minnesota.

102024
012025

THIS BOOK CONTAINS RECYCLED MATERIALS

Cover Photo: NASA
Interior Photos: Getty Images, NASA, Shutterstock Images
Editor: Grace Hansen
Series Designer: Victoria Bates

Library of Congress Control Number: 2024938580

Publisher's Cataloging-in-Publication Data
Names: Andrews, Elizabeth, author.
Title: Asteroids & meteors / by Elizabeth Andrews
Description: Minneapolis, Minnesota : Pop!, 2025 | Series: Space objects | Includes online resources and index
Identifiers: ISBN 9781098246952 (lib. bdg.) | ISBN 9781098247515 (ebook)
Subjects: LCSH: Outer space--Exploration--Juvenile literature. | Asteroids--Juvenile literature. | Solar system--Juvenile literature. | Astronomy--Juvenile literature. | Universe--Juvenile literature.
Classification: DDC 523.6--dc23

Table of Contents

Chapter 1
The Solar System 4

Chapter 2
Asteroids. 8

Chapter 3
Meteoroids & Meteors 12

Chapter 4
Famous Asteroids. 20

Making Connections 22
Glossary 23
Index. 24
Online Resources 24

Chapter 1

The Solar System

Our **solar system** was formed around 4.6 billion years ago. **Gravity** pulled together gas and dust to create the Sun. Space objects such as asteroids were formed from leftover gas and dust.

Our solar system is made up of the Sun, eight planets, and thousands of other smaller objects.

Watch a video here!

Asteroids and meteors are the rocky remains of the materials that formed the solar system. They are irregularly shaped.

Humans can see asteroids and meteors with a telescope.

Chapter 2

Asteroids

Long ago, a cloud of dust and gas **orbited** the Sun. The materials **collided** to become large pieces of rock and metal. Some of the largest pieces became planets. Smaller pieces became asteroids.

Millions of asteroids orbit the Sun.
Learn more here!

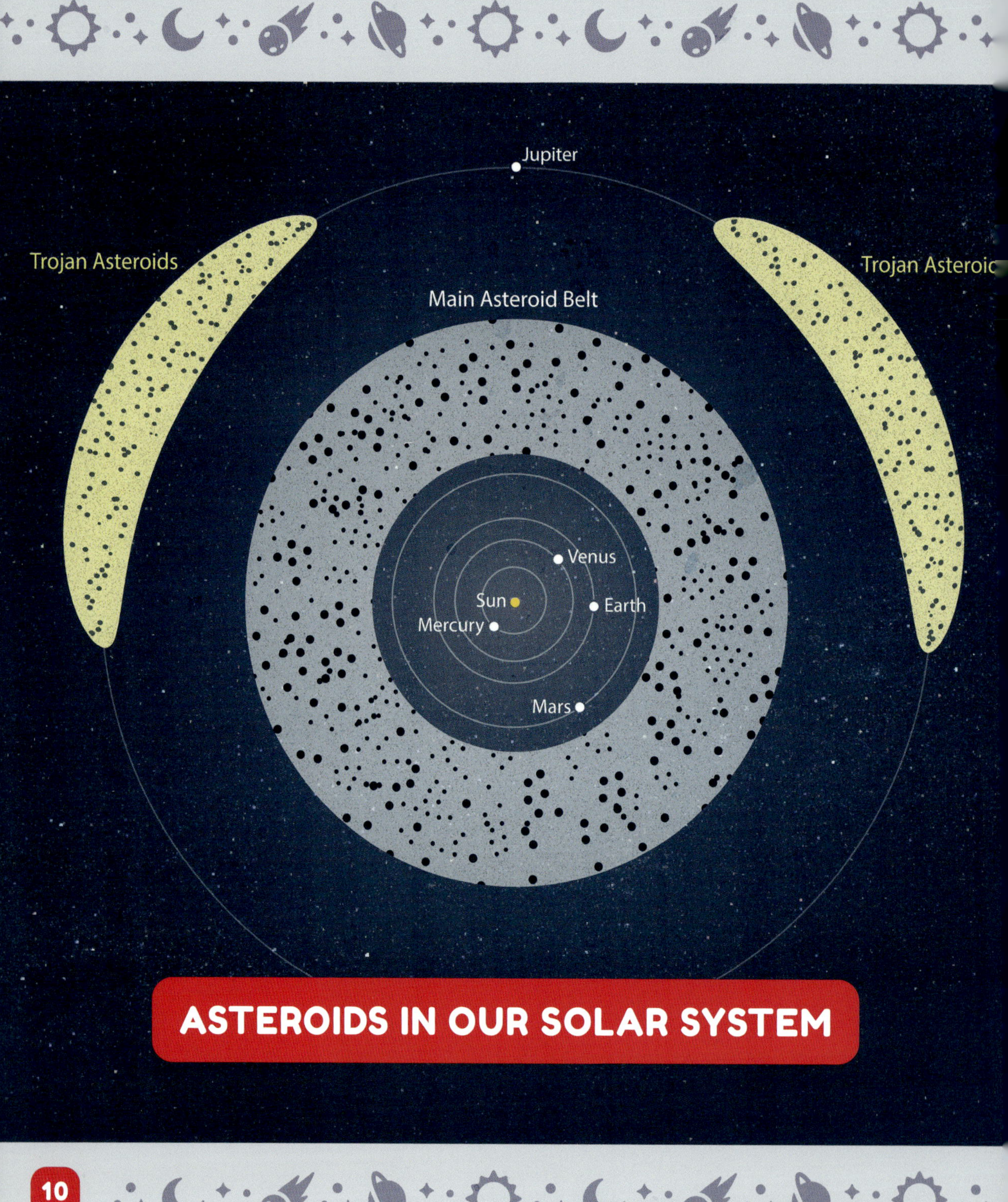
Jupiter
Trojan Asteroids
Trojan Asteroic
Main Asteroid Belt
Venus
Sun
Earth
Mercury
Mars
ASTEROIDS IN OUR SOLAR SYSTEM

Most asteroids are in the main belt between Mars and Jupiter. Some are outside the belt. Trojan asteroids share an orbit with Jupiter. There are more asteroids throughout our solar system.

Chapter 3

Meteoroids & Meteors

Asteroids can be hundreds of miles wide or just a few feet. Meteoroids are smaller pieces of asteroids that break away after **collisions**. They are often the size of a fist.

Explore links here!

Asteroids can hit the Earth as well. They are much bigger and can cause extreme damage.

Earth's **gravity** can pull meteoroids into its **atmosphere**. The meteoroid moves very fast creating **friction**, heat, and quick flashes of light. This is a meteor. It can also be called a shooting star.

Most meteors burn up after entering the atmosphere. Some reach the Earth's surface. These are called meteorites.

Sometimes Earth moves through large groups of meteoroids. Many meteors

enter the atmosphere all at once. This creates a meteor shower.

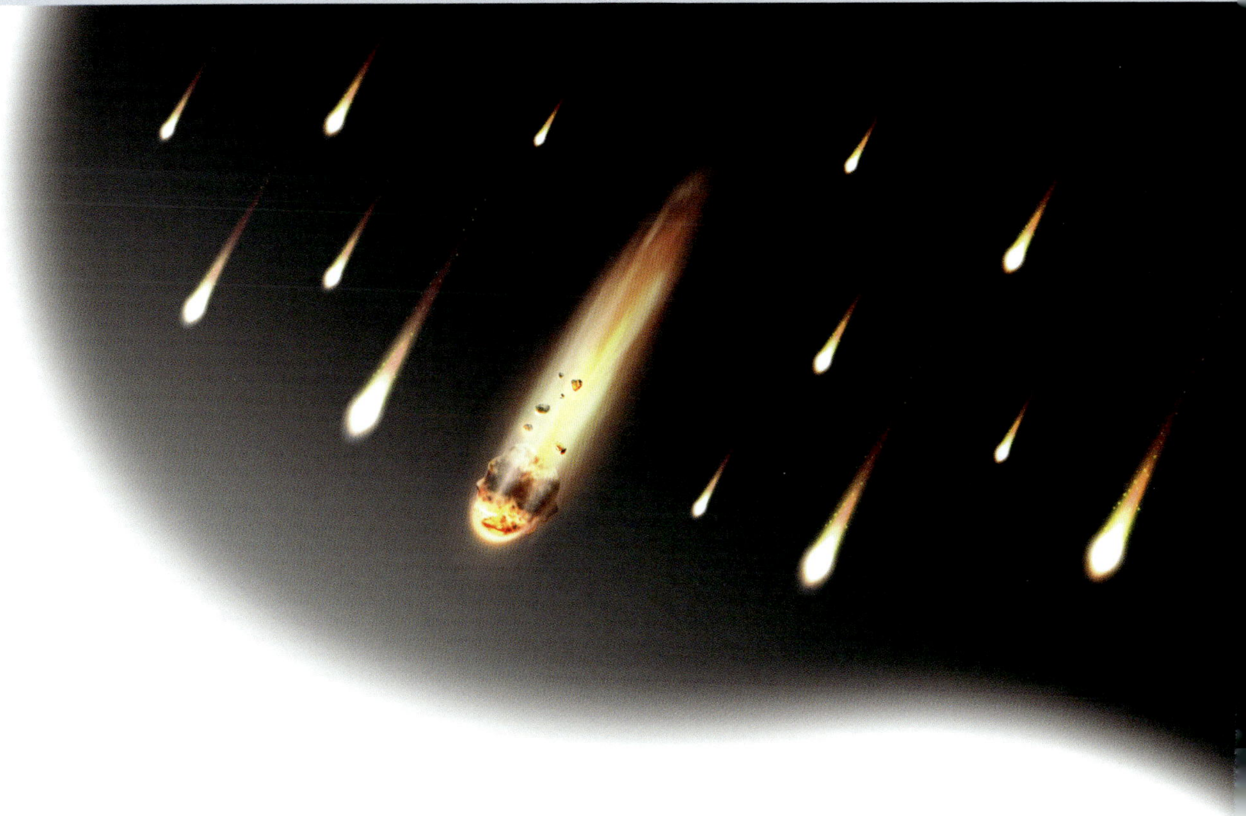

The Chelyabinsk Meteorite hit Earth in November 2013. It weighs 1,190 lbs (540kg).

About 50,000 meteorites have been discovered on Earth. Scientists study them to learn where the pieces of space rock came from. Other space objects, such as planets and moons, get hit by meteorites too.

Chapter 4

Famous Asteroids

The asteroid Vesta is 329 miles (530km) wide. It is thought to be the second largest asteroid in the main belt. Scientists have sent spacecraft to explore Vesta. Ceres is the largest asteroid.

Complete an activity here!

Scientists believe that a large asteroid hit Earth 66 million years ago and wiped out most of the dinosaurs and many other animals.

Making Connections

Text-to-Self

How would you prepare to watch a meteor shower? Think about where you would go, who you would bring with, and what supplies you would need.

Text-to-Text

Have you read any books about other space objects? If so, how were those objects similar to or different from asteroids and meteors?

Text-to-World

With the help of an adult, look up a historical meteor impact on Earth. Write a few sentences describing what you learned about the impact.

Glossary

atmosphere – a protective layer of gas around an object in space.

collision – the act of coming together with force; crash. Objects that collide are in a collision.

friction – the rubbing of bodies against each other.

gravity – a force that pulls objects toward each other.

orbit – the path of a space object as it moves around another space object. To orbit is to follow this path.

solar system – any system that includes a star and all of the matter which orbits that star, including planets and moons.

Index

atmosphere, 15–17
Earth, 15–16, 19
gravity, 4, 15
main belt, 11, 20
meteorites, 16, 19
meteoroid, 12, 15
orbit, 8, 11
solar system, 4, 6, 11
telescope, 7
Trojan asteroids, 11
Vesta, 20

Online Resources

popbooksonline.com

Thanks for reading this Cody Koala book!

This book is filled with videos, puzzles, games, and more! Scan the QR codes* while you read, or visit the website below to make this book pop.

popbooksonline.com/ast-met

*Scanning QR codes requires a web-enabled smart device with a QR code reader app and a camera.